AMER

WE MUST NOT FORGET

A Patriotic Call for Revival in America

CREATED BY
MIKE HARLAND WITH CHRIS MACHEN
AND LUKE GARRETT

ARRANGED AND ORCHESTRATED BY
RICHARD KINGSMORE

Products Available:

Choral Book	0-6330-8919-2
Listening Cassette	0-6330-8921-4
Listening CD	0-6330-8920-6
Accompaniment CD	0-6330-8922-2
(Split track and Instruments only)	
Cassette Promo Pack	0-6330-8931-1
CD Promo Pack	0-6330-8923-0
Rehearsal Tracks	0-6330-8926-5
Poster	0-6330-8928-1
Bulletins (pack of 100)	0-6330-8927-3
DVD	0-6330-8924-9

GENEVOX

AMERICA
WE MUST NOT FORGET

A Patriotic Call for Revival in America

This is an opportune time in our nation's history for the church to build bridges in local communities. Although the DVD and production notes are valuable resources, your presentation will have its greatest impact as you customize it for your community. We encourage you to use *America, We Must Not Forget* to honor local civic leaders and other public servants, and to strengthen your region's entire church community as you recognize unsung heroes in its spiritual life. Consider ways to make *America, We Must Not Forget* part of your local observance of national holidays. The opportunity to reach your world may never be greater.

Genevox is pleased to offer our second DVD project. *America, We Must Not Forget* DVD takes full advantage of the capabilities of this medium. The video stream includes footage that brings the three sections of this musical to life. Projectable song texts are included at moments when congregational participation seems appropriate.

The audio stream offers a split-track mix. Additional audio options are available to those using a 5.1 player, including a click track that the conductor can use to synchronize live music with visual images, a rhythm-only mix, a brass-and-woodwind mix, a string-only mix, a vocal-only mix, and a complete studio recording with narration.

Refer to the inside back cover of this choral book for information about our first Genevox DVD product: *Jesus, the One and Only.*

Foreword

LUKE GARRETT

MIKE HARLAND

RICHARD KINGSMORE

CHRIS MACHEN

WE consider it an incredible honor to preser *America, We Must Not Forget* to you. The moments of these pages have been felt and experienced in our heart as we have reflected on recent events in our country and our current war on terrorism.

Following the terrorists' attacks of September 11, 2001, a common statement could be seen on bumper stickers and banners, at ball games and parades. That statement was: "We will never forget." There is no doubt that we will never forget that we were attacked by an enemy resolute to see our demise as a nation. But are there other things America must never forget?

In the concept stage of this work we asked that question, and the answer came back a resounding, "Yes The result is what you hold in your hand.

America must never forget our heritage as a Christi nation, or those who gave and still give to protect our fre dom and our spiritual strength. But, most of all, we must not forget that our only hope is in Almighty God.

We are proud to present this work that honors America, but also cries out to God for revival in this land that we love.

God have mercy on us.

CONTENTS

Prologue

Arranged by Richard Kingsn

*These index points reference the DVD as well as the accompaniment CD. On the DVD, the first index point
each song is located at the beginning of the click track count-off. Those using other mixes will note a delay in t
instrumental entrances. It is possible to present the musical in its entirety without pausing the DVD unless
necessitated by audience response.

"God, Have Mercy," Music by Mike Harland, Chris Machen, and Luke Garrett.
© Copyright 2002 Van Ness Press, Inc. (ASCAP).

"O God, Our Help in Ages Past"

8

11

Let the Words of Freedom Ring

Words and Musi
MIKE HARLAND and LUKE GARR
Arranged by Richard Kingsr

*NARRATION
America-what a heritage of freedom! Throughout the history of these United States, there
been great men and women whose words have inspired us to live as free people. Those w
are more than historical fact; they remain great inspiration. We come once again to le
words of freedom ring!

14

let the__ words__ of free-dom ring.

*VOICE 1: "It is rather for us to be here dedicated to the great task remaining before us . . . this nation, under God, shall have a new birth of freedom - and that government of the pec by the people, for the people, shall not perish from the earth."

Abraham Lincoln from the Gettysburg Add

*These quotations may be delivered by the narrator, by offstage voices, or by costumed characters on the stage.

new birth of freedom..."

Oboe

⑨

"...from the earth."

We learned the words_ from those who've gone be -

VOICE 2: "We hold these truths to be self-evident, that all men are created equal."

Declaration of Indepen

VOICE 3: "I know not what course others may take; but as for me, give me liberty, or give me death!"

Patrick H

VOICE 4: "It cannot be emphasized too strongly or too often that this great nation w founded, not by religionists, but by Christians; not on religions, but on the gospel of Je Christ."

Patrick H

VOICE 5: "The course of this conflict is not known, yet its outcome is certain. Freedom and justice and cruelty, have always been at war, and we know that God is not neutral between them."

George W.

"My Country, 'Tis of Thee," Music: *Thesaurus Musicus*, 1744.
Arr. © Copyright 2002 Van Ness Press, Inc. (ASCAP).

Underscore - We Pledge Allegiance

Arranged by Richard Kingsmore

ARRATION (*upbeat and energetic*)

, let the words of freedom ring! Let them fill the hearts of every American and every person t longs to live in freedom. That's what this celebration is all about! And now we rise, like all :riots who love liberty, to say just thirty-one words of freedom holding so much meaning for Americans. It starts with "I," which means just one, but ends with "all," and that means ry one of us. These words honor the flag that has flown across the world representing our 'ublic. They pledge our loyalty and express our total dependence on our God. In recent 's, some of these words have come under attack. But now we will say them proudly once 1in. Please stand as we say the Pledge of Allegiance:

pledge Allegiance to the flag of the United States of America and to the Republic for which it nds, one nation under God, indivisible, with Liberty and Justice for all."

d now, join us in singing our national anthem.

lectively (♩ = 84)

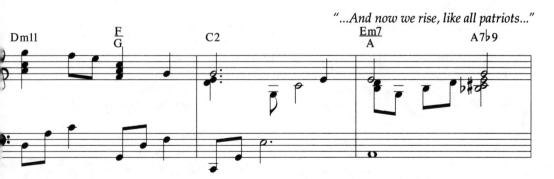

nerica the Beautiful," Music by Samuel A. Ward.

"...but ends with 'all,'..."

"...and express our total..."

"Please stand as we say the Pledge..."

(Segue to "The Star-Spangled Bann

rit.

The Star-Spangled Banner

Words by FRANCIS SCOTT KEY

Music from unknown source;
Attributed to JOHN STAFFORD SMITH
Arranged by Richard Kingsmore

home of the brave, the home of the

brave?

Underscore - We Must Not Forget

Arranged by Richard Kingsmo

*NARRATION (*solemn*)
Through our history, there have been those among us rise up to pay the price of freedom.
know many of their names: men like George Washington, Patrick Henry; women like Be
Ross and Dolly Madison. They and many others are the heroes of colonial America. But th
courage was not unique. Through the years, there have been Americans who answered the c
of our country: Clara Barton, Alvin York and Douglas McArthur, Norman Schwarzkopf a
Christa McAuliffe, to name a few. Some have been ordinary citizens thrust into the front lir
for our country. They include men like Todd Beamer, whose words, "Let's roll," on Septeml
11, 2001, became a battle cry for our nation. We must never forget their courage a
selflessness. But for every name we know, there are countless unknown countrymen a
women who defended freedom. Not all of them died for our cause, but all were willing to. '
must always remember and honor those who have stood at the gates of our cities for us.

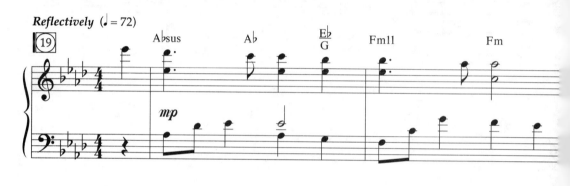

"Now Thank We All Our God,"Music: Johann Cruger; harm. Felix Mendelssohn.
Arr. © Copyright 2002 Van Ness Press, Inc. (ASCAP).

Sea of Glory
with *America the Beautiful*

Words and Musi
MIKE HARLAND and LUKE GARR
Arranged by Richard Kingsn

"...at the gates of our cities for us."

38

LADIES

Through the years we've de - fend - ed hon - or,

and to - day we will fight for hon - or.

How can we____ do an - y less for A -

43

"America the Beautiful," Words by Katherine Lee Bates; Music by Samuel A. Ward.

DVD includes video enhancement of the following narration prior to the instrumental introduction.
ing should be carefully rehearsed.

We Salute Our Heroes

Arranged by Richard Kingsmore

ARRATION *(begins without music)*

ery generation has produced its own heroes: men and women who have defended freedom
d confronted wrong wherever it has been found. Not all of our heroes fought in military
mpaigns. *The terrorist attacks of 2001 reminded us all how we depend on our fellow citizens
protect, defend, and serve so that we can live in freedom. These are the people who run into
ldings that you and I run out of. They stand ready at a moment's notice to come to our aid.
uld those of you who serve as law enforcement, or firefighters, or any other emergency
rsonnel, please stand so that we may honor you? *(pause)* Please be seated.

me of our heroes paid the ultimate price for the freedom we enjoy. Jesus himself said,
reater love hath no man than this, that a man lay down his life for his friends" (John 15:13,
V). If you have lost a family member in the line of duty, or in defense of our country, or in
tecting the well-being of our fellow citizens, please stand. *(pause)* You may be seated.

 also want to show our thanks to those among us who have fought on this nation's battle
nts or who have kept the peace around the world. As we call out each campaign, we ask all
you who served in the Army, Navy, Air Force, Marines, Coast Guard, or National Guard to
ase stand and remain standing, so that we may honor you.

rld War I, World War II, Korean Conflict, Vietnam War, Grenada, The Gulf War-Operation
sert Storm, Afghanistan-Operation Enduring Freedom, and Peacekeeping Forces.

d now, a little flag waving if you please!

so that we may honor you..."   *"...Please be seated."*

Still, My Soul," Music: Jean Sibelius.

50

"Taps," Music: Daniel Adams Butterfield.

"*...You may be seated.*"   (*pay tribute to those who served our country in various conflicts*)

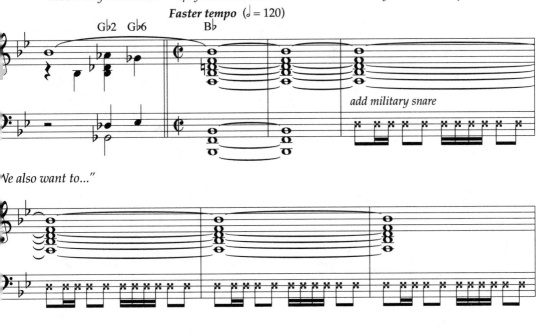

"*We also want to...*"

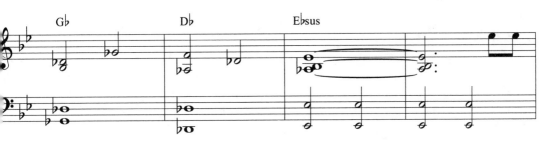

"*The Stars and Stripes Forever*"
(*narration continues*)
"*As we call out...*"

"The Stars and Stripes Forever," Music: John Philip Sousa.

"...so that we may honor you."

54

56

Song for the Heroes

Words and Music
MIKE HARLAND, CHRIS MACHEN, and LUKE GARRI
Arranged by Richard Kingsm

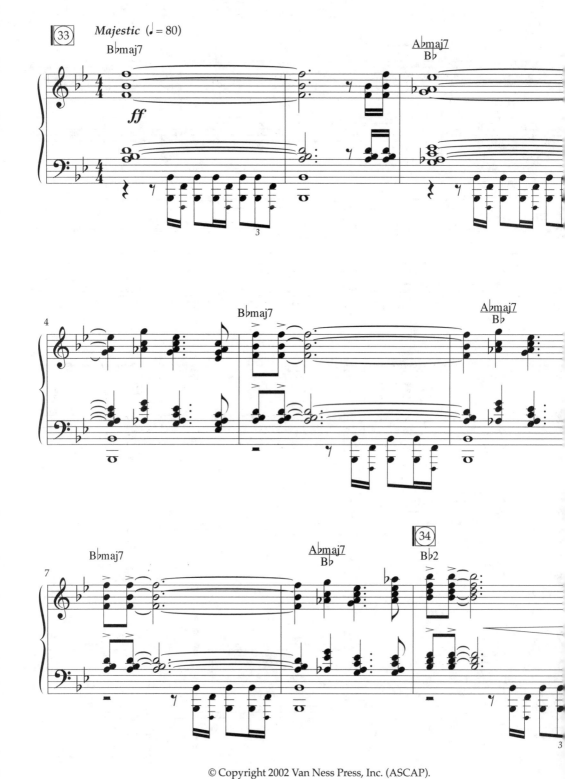

CODA

lost.

Some fought in for - eign lands,

and some re - mained be - hind. But

all have soared as ea - gles, de - fend - ing free - dom's

66

68

Underscore -
Battle Hymn of the Republic

Arranged by Richard Kingsm

*NARRATION

Just as there have been those who have fought for the freedom of our country, there have
those who have fought for the soul of it. Since the beginning, we have been "one nation u
God." These are the men and women who have fought on an unseen battlefield
nonetheless, protected the integrity and honor of this nation. Men like Jonathan Edwards
Dwight L. Moody, and, today, Dr. James Dobson, Dr. D. James Kennedy, and many others.
in all of modern America, who can measure the influence for good and for God that Dr.
Graham has had on presidents and on the people? After the terrorist attacks of 2001, v
America was at one of its lowest moments, it was Dr. Graham who spoke as a pastor to the na

Why has God blessed our nation with godly leaders and spiritual heroes in every genera
How is it that our country has known His favor and blessing? America was born under
providence to give testimony of His greatness. It's not that we deserve His blessing, it's tha
desires for all people around the world to know Him. God has revealed the reason He p
out His favor on a nation. It is as the Bible says in Isaiah 41 "that people may see and k
may consider and understand, that the hand of the Lord has done this" (v. 20). God has ble
America (*"Our God Reigns on High" begins*) so that we can be a light to the world. It's tim
stand and proclaim it: God is our God, and He reigns on high!

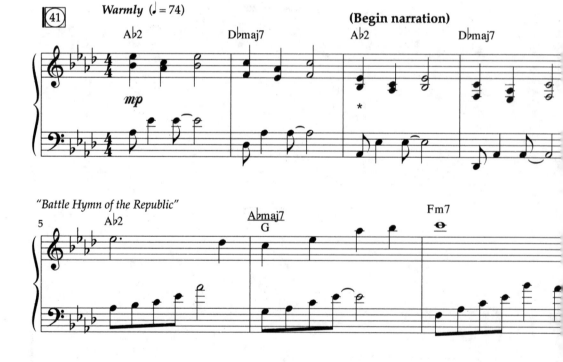

"Battle Hymn of the Republic," Music: American Folk Song, 19th C.

Narration will continue beyond this underscore.

Our God Reigns on High

with *Battle Hymn of the Republic*

Words and Musi
MIKE HARLAND and LUKE GARR
Arranged by Richard Kingsn

74

we must__ de-clare, as long as__ we're here, that

Bb   Bbno3   Bb   Bbno3
                     Ab   Ab

our God reigns on high._____

Eb Ebmaj7 Fsus Eb   Bb   Bbsus
G   G   F

FEMALE SOLO *mf*

It's   time to__ de-clare to__ the

C   Csus   C2

mf

Add FEMALE on bottom-harmony

free - dom were not a - shamed of___ the gos - pel__ of

Ah____

Christ. So let us call on__ His name and re -

Call on__ His

"Battle Hymn of the Republic"

le Hymn of the Republic," Words by Julia Ward Howe; Music: Amer. Folk Song, 19th C.
© Copyright 2002 Van Ness Press, Inc. (ASCAP)

89

O God, Our Help in Ages Past

Words by ISAAC WATTS

**Music by WILLIAM CR(
Arranged by Richard Kingsm

NARRATION (*begins without music*)

We've been reminded of our heritage and that the very founding documents of this rep
proclaim our belief in a sovereign God and that we exist to serve Him. We've remembere
heroes of our history and those with us today that defend and protect the liberty we know
have also given thanks for those who have fought and for those who are fighting for the sc
our nation. But what is our hope for tomorrow?

"...We have also given thanks..."

**New Words and Music by Mike Harland.

God, Have Mercy

Words and Mus
MIKE HARLAND, CHRIS MACHEN and LUKE GARI
Arranged by Richard Kings

*The text provided here and during "Season of Prayer" at measure 66 comes from the studio recor
and serves only as a model for pastors to lead in a time of repentance and rededication.*

*"If my people, which are called by my name, shall humble themselves, and pray, and
my face, and turn from their wicked ways; then will I hear from heaven, and will forgive
sin, and heal their land" (2 Chron. 7:14, KJV).

How many times have we heard these words, thinking they will change America if
would only believe them? But these words were not intended to challenge our nation.
they were spoken by God to His chosen people. Today it's a call to the people of God—
church—to come to Him in repentance, to confess our sins, to humble ourselves before Hi

** *Prayer (meas. 66)*

It's time to come to the altar before God Almighty and pray like you've never pra
before. Pray for yourself, pray for the church, pray for America.

Merciful God, we praise Your name. We come before You as Your people to confess our
You have been faithful when we have been faithless. You have loved us with an everlas
love, even when we have failed to love You. We've taken for granted our freedom to wors
freedom that men and women have died for. When challenged to stand for righteousn
we've often turned a deaf ear and looked the other way. We have kept silent when we c
have shared the greatest news of all: the gospel of Jesus Christ. Forgive us, Lord! We do
Your face because we know that only You can heal our land.

Almighty God, we intercede on behalf of our president and his cabinet. We pray that
senators, our congressmen and women, and all of our community leaders will wal
integrity and govern with godly wisdom. If ever we needed Your mercy and grace, O L
it's right now. Turn our hearts, turn Your people, turn this nation back to You. O God,
mercy on us!

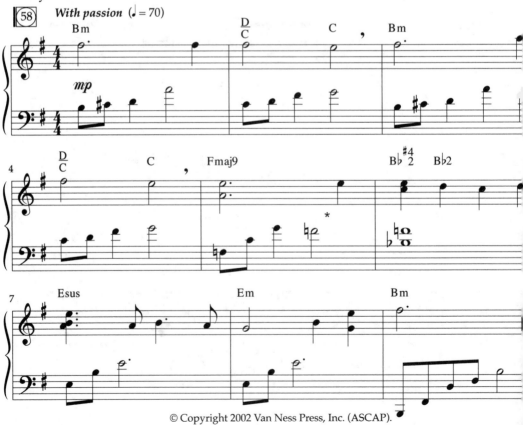

umble ourselves before Him..."

softly, but with intensity

God,   have

"Season of Prayer"
**(Begin Narration-prayer)

Let us be a ho-ly na - tion.

By Your pow - er and for Your glo - ry,———

Make us be a ho-ly na - tion.

112

114

Pray for America

Words and Music by
MIKE HARLAND and LUKE GARRETT
Arranged by Richard Kingsmore

FEMALE SOLO

At her birth,— this na-tion knew— the hand of God.— "I

God we trust,"— was more than just— a phrase.

116

God has prom-ised He would hear a nation's cry. His mer-cy, free, still far ex-ceeds our

122

God would shed His grace on thee. And as we

Dbmaj7   Dbm6/Fb   Dbm6   Dbm6/Bb

pray for A-mer - i - ca, we stay for A-mer - i - ca,___ be -

Ab2   Gb/Ab

fore His sov-'reign hand, on our knees.___ From

Dbmaj7   Ab2/C   Gb2   Gb

124

pray for A-mer-i-ca, pray for A-mer-i-ca that

God would shed His grace_____ on thee; That

God would shed His grace on thee.

Finale

Arranged by Richard Kingsmore

NARRATION (*prior to music or on-screen images*)
God has blessed the United States of America. But we must not take His blessings for granted. The dependence of our founding fathers on our Heavenly Father brought His blessing on the beginnings of our country. The faithful men and women who have called upon Him have sustained His grace among us. Beyond that, God Himself, for His own purposes, placed us among the greatest nations in the history of the world. We must never forget the heritage of our dependence on God. We should pray as Defense Secretary Donald Rumsfeld prayed on September 14, 2001: "Not that God will be on our side, *(Finale begins)* *but always, O Lord, that America will be on your side." We must never forget our heroes and their sacrifices on our behalf. But, most of all, we must never forget that our only hope for survival is for our nation to turn to the God who made us what we are and call upon Him to heal our land. America, we must not forget!

132

"Let the Words of Freedom Ring"

Let the__ words__ of free-dom

ring.

Let the__ words__ of free-dom

138

"Sea of Glory," Words and Music by Mike Harland and Luke Garrett.
© Copyright 2002 Van Ness Press, Inc. (ASCAP).

AMERICA

WE MUST NOT FORGET

PRODUCTION NOTES

By Debbie Beavers

Prologue

Enlist members of the armed forces, law enforcement officers, firefighters, paramedics, and other civil servants from your congregation or your city/town to participate in a processional of personnel and the color guard. To ensure representation throughout the room, have participants enter in random order to fill the aisles of your sanctuary. Use the outside aisles and, if necessary, use the area in front of the first row of seats, then other aisles. Leave the center aisle and access to the stage clear. Based on the size of your sanctuary and the number of persons involved, the processional can begin with "O God, Our Help in Ages Past" (meas. 34) or "America, We Must Not Forget" (meas. 50).

PART ONE:
We Remember Our Heritage

"Let the Words of Freedom Ring"

The congregation should stand as the color guard processional begins at measure 73. The color guard should enter and process down the center aisle, reaching center stage on the platform by the end of the song. If you prefer to have the color guard enter in silence, stop the DVD at the end of the song, then begin the DVD once they are in place on the platform.

"Underscore—We Pledge Allegiance" and "The Star-Spangled Banner"

Processional participants remain in their positions. At the conclusion of "The Star-Spangled Banner," stop the DVD to allow for the color guard recessional. The congregation should also be seated.

PART TWO:
We Remember Our Heroes

"Sea of Glory"

Enlist one child for each processional participant. These children will present a gift or token of appreciation during this song. They can present roses, plaques, or mementos prepared by children in Sunday School. There are many creative ways to honor these individuals. As the choir begins the first chorus, participants standing in the outside aisles should turn and file to the platform. They should form one or two lines, depending on the number enlisted. They should be staggered across the platform so that each one is visible. Leave enough space for a child to stand beside each person. If the platform is not large enough, use the steps leading up to the platform and the area in between the platform and the first row of seats. As the ladies begin the second stanza, the children should begin processing slowly down the center aisle. The entrance of each child should be spaced as many as 10 rows apart. This will depend on the number of children and the size of your sanctuary. The children should present their gift, then stand beside that person. If all children are in place, begin the recessional at the coda; otherwise, begin at measure 68. Each pair should recess hand in hand, and they should be spaced as many as 10 rows apart as they exit.

"We Salute Our Heroes"

This is a different approach to recognizing those who have served our country. Each congregation will be different. The narration and images on the DVD cover military conflicts from World War I to the present. You can modify the narration to better reflect the makeup and response of your congregation. The DVD is intended to enhance the recognition of these veterans.

"Song for the Heroes"

Ask church members to bring photos of loved ones who died while serving in the line of duty. These photos will be placed on the altar during this song. Also include those who have family members currently serving in the line of duty. Persons with photos should slowly make their way to the platform at the beginning of the coda. Have them alternate their movement to the platform; they should not all move at once. If you are not using the DVD, prepare a PowerPoint presentation of these photos to use during this song.

"Our God Reigns on High"

This song is a congregational participation piece. If you are not using the DVD, prepare a PowerPoint presentation of the lyrics beginning at measure 79 through the end of the song.

PART THREE:
We Remember Our Hope

"O God, Our Help in Ages Past"

This song is a congregational participation piece. If you are not using the DVD, prepare a PowerPoint presentation of the lyrics for the first two verses. There should be no lyrics for the bridge (measures 67-82) or the solo.

"God, Have Mercy"

Enlist deacons, staff members, military personnel, or couples with children currently serving in the military to lead a candlelight service. As the choir begins to sing, the candlelighters should enter from the back and slowly process down the aisles to the front. At measure 39, begin lighting the congregational candles. Candles remain lit through the end of the song. This song will provide a time for the congregation to spend in prayer at the altar or in their seats. The suggested prayer is merely a model. The pastor should "make it his own," tailoring it to the needs of your congregation.

"Pray for America"

Members of your congregation may still be at the altar. This song should be an extension of the opportunity to kneel at the altar. It will also provide a time for the congregation to transition from an emotional mood to a celebrative mood.

Finale

Have those who serve our nation in some capacity to reenter the sanctuary, display the flag, or both.

General Note: As you block the movements of the narrator, use the entire sanctuary.

—Debbie Beavers is a Video Producer, Publishing Services and Multimedia, LifeWay Church Resources. She produced the video portion of the companion DVD for America, We Must Not Forget. She has a master's degree in communication from Southwestern Baptist Theological Seminary, Fort Worth, Texas. She has 20 years of experience in writing and directing pageantry and church drama in churches of all sizes.